Want more leadership ideas and tools
or info about my CEO Group?
Check out www.theBESTCEOgroup.com.

You're Crazy! How the Hell Are We Going to Do That?!

What Leaders Need to Do to Be Successful and Get Their People Really Engaged and Fully Committed

Joe Phillips

THiNK*aha*®

An Actionable Business Journal

E-mail: info@thinkaha.com
20660 Stevens Creek Blvd., Suite 210
Cupertino, CA 95014

Published by THiNKaha®
20660 Stevens Creek Blvd., Suite 210, Cupertino, CA 95014
http://thinkaha.com
E-mail: info@thinkaha.com

First Printing: November 2018
Hardcover ISBN: 978-1-61699-287-3   1-61699-287-5
Paperback ISBN: 978-1-61699-286-6   1-61699-286-7
eBook ISBN: 978-1-61699-285-9   1-61699-285-9
Place of Publication: Silicon Valley, California, USA
Paperback Library of Congress Number: 2018957955

Trademarks

All terms mentioned in this book that are known to be trademarks or service marks have been appropriately capitalized. Neither THiNKaha, nor any of its imprints, can attest to the accuracy of this information. Use of a term in this book should not be regarded as affecting the validity of any trademark or service mark.

Warning and Disclaimer

Every effort has been made to make this book as complete and as accurate as possible. The information provided is on an "as is" basis. The author(s), publisher, and their agents assume no responsibility for errors or omissions. Nor do they assume liability or responsibility to any person or entity with respect to any loss or damages arising from the use of information contained herein.

Acknowledgements

I would like to acknowledge the CEOs who have been in my Group for all they have taught me and the trust they have had in me. In particular, I would like to thank the eight CEOs who have spent more than ten years as participants in the Group and who had patience with me in the early days when I was learning how to be effective as a chair.

Dedication

I'm dedicating this book to my wife of fifty-one years, Judith R. Phillips, PhD. She has been my life-long supporter and my inspiration because of her dedication, fierce work ethic, and full commitment to the things she undertakes.

How to Read a THiNKaha® Book

A Note from the Publisher

The AHAthat/THiNKaha series is the CliffsNotes of the 21st century. These books are contextual in nature. Although the actual words won't change, their meaning will every time you read one as your context will change. Be ready, you will experience your own AHA moments as you read the AHA messages™ in this book. They are designed to be stand-alone actionable messages that will help you think about a project you're working on, an event, a sales deal, a personal issue, etc. differently. As you read this book, please think about the following:

1. It should only take 15-20 minutes to read this book the first time out. When you're reading, write in the underlined area one to three action items that resonate with you.
2. Mark your calendar to re-read this book again in 30 days.
3. Repeat step #1 and mark one to three more AHA messages that resonate. They will most likely be different than the first time. BTW: this is also a great time to reflect on the AHAmessages that resonated with you during your last reading.

After reading a THiNKaha book, marking your AHA messages, re-reading it, and marking more AHA messages, you'll begin to see how these books contextually apply to you. AHAthat/THiNKaha books advocate for continuous, lifelong learning. They will help you transform your AHAs into actionable items with tangible results until you no longer have to say AHA to these moments—they'll become part of your daily practice as you continue to grow and learn.

Mitchell Levy, The AHA Guy at AHAthat
publisher@thinkaha.com

THiNKaha®

Contents

Contents

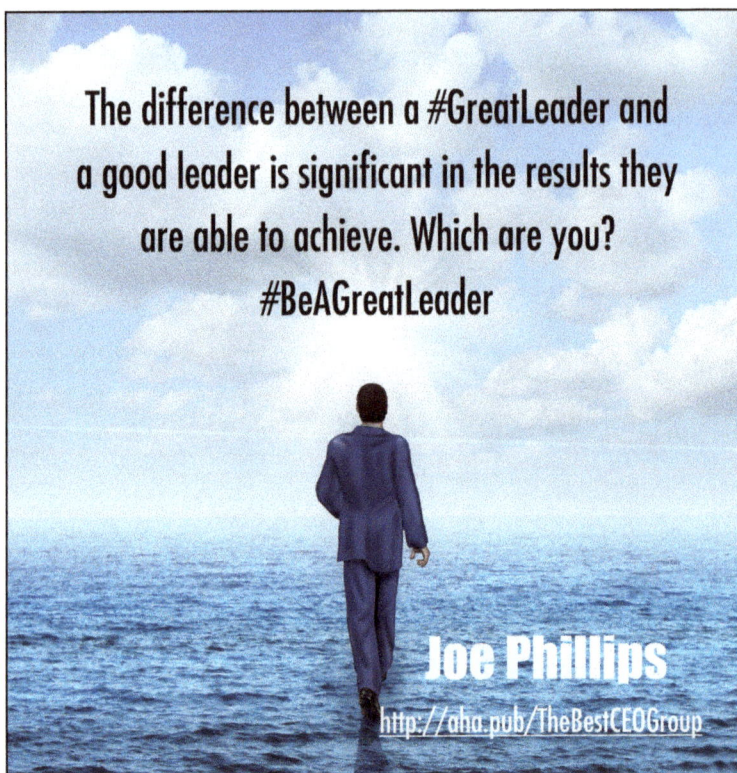

The difference between a #GreatLeader and a good leader is significant in the results they are able to achieve. Which are you? #BeAGreatLeader

Joe Phillips

http://aha.pub/TheBestCEOGroup

Share the AHA messages from this book socially by going to
http://aha.pub/TheBestCEOGroup

Section I

Great Leadership Is
a Killer Differentiator

There's a big difference between a good leader and a great leader. Not only does this difference affect everyone in the organization, but it also affects the success of the company. A great leader is one who puts the organization and their employees first, rather than themselves. They make sure their organization is built on trust and respect.

Great leaders are great communicators. They know that people don't like uncertainty—when it exists, they assume the worst. So, they communicate with their team often. Foremost, they communicate the vision and values for the business. They are exceptionally competent, fully committed, and work harder than almost anyone but empower others to take on as much as they are capable. Great leaders see the big picture and work on their business more than they work in it.

1

Read and share "You're Crazy! How the Hell Are We Going to Do That?" on social media by going to http://aha.pub/YoureCrazy. http://aha.pub/JoePhillips #GreatLeaders

_____

_____

_____

2

#GreatLeaders know what really excites their people about what they do and what makes them most proud of being part of the company. http://aha.pub/JoePhillips

_____

_____

_____

3

#GreatLeaders are effective communicators! They communicate their vision, challenges, and where the business truly stands. http://aha.pub/JoePhillips

_____

_____

_____

4

CEOs need to #Communicate the things their employees need to hear, not just what they want to say. #GreatLeaders http://aha.pub/JoePhillips

_____

_____

_____

5

#GreatLeaders are honest and tell the truth; they don't sugar-coat things. Do you? http://aha.pub/JoePhillips

_____

_____

_____

6

Uncertainty is a demotivator for employees. If you don't tell them what's going on, they'll imagine the worst. #GreatLeaders
http://aha.pub/JoePhillips

_____

_____

_____

7

#GreatLeaders are more concerned about the business and the organization than about themselves.
http://aha.pub/JoePhillips

_____

_____

_____

8

1 of 5 Attributes of #GreatLeaders: They can inspire their teams to execute on plans. http://aha.pub/JoePhillips

_____

_____

_____

9

2 of 5 Attributes of #GreatLeaders: They have a powerful vision that they and their team are fully committed to. http://aha.pub/JoePhillips

_____

_____

_____

10

3 of 5 Attributes of #GreatLeaders: They achieve performance through helping people have insights versus telling. http://aha.pub/JoePhillips

---

11

4 of 5 Attributes of #GreatLeaders: They have a heart and show it through their actions. http://aha.pub/JoePhillips

---

12

5 of 5 Attributes of #GreatLeaders: They
are humble and have a fierce resolve.
—Jim Collins via http://aha.pub/JoePhillips

_____

_____

_____

13

#GreatLeaders spend far more time focusing on the future than the average leader. http://aha.pub/JoePhillips

_____

_____

_____

14

#GreatLeaders are adamant about continuous improvement. Good is never good enough for the really important things. http://aha.pub/JoePhillips

_____

_____

_____

15

The difference between a #GreatLeader and a good leader is significant in the results they are able to achieve. Which are you? #BeAGreatLeader
http://aha.pub/JoePhillips

_____

_____

_____

If you feel that your goals are realistic and obtainable, put them out there and help your employees figure out how to achieve them.
#GreatLeaders

Joe Phillips
http://aha.pub/TheBestCEOGroup

Share the AHA messages from this book socially by going to
http://aha.pub/TheBestCEOGroup

Section II

Why Challenging Your Team Gets You Big Gains

People and organizations don't perform up to their potential if they are comfortable where they are. So, the leader's job is to make their team uncomfortable. The best way to do this is to get the team to accept big, hairy, audacious goals, both in vision and yearly growth. Some experts recommend 10× growth. This way, the team will know that they will not be able to get there with luck or by working just a little harder. It will take a significant change in how they operate.

Also, it's better to make 85 percent of a really challenging goal than 100 percent of a conservative one. By achieving 85 percent, your team will see that they accomplished more than they initially thought was realistic and will be more open for bigger challenges going forward.

16

If employees aren't saying, "How the hell are we going to do that?", you're not being the #GreatLeader you can be. http://aha.pub/JoePhillips

_____

_____

_____

17

You can't continue to operate the way you've been operating and achieve really big goals. #GreatLeaders http://aha.pub/JoePhillips

_____

_____

_____

18

The 10× Rule: Look to take your business 10× in a specific area from where it is today. #GreatLeaders @GrantCardone via http://aha.pub/JoePhillips https://goo.gl/GhqvCW

_____

_____

_____

19

Does your team think exponentially beyond the customer base you have today? #GreatLeaders http://aha.pub/JoePhillips

_____

_____

_____

20

If you feel that your goals are realistic and obtainable, put them out there and help your employees figure out how to achieve them. #GreatLeaders http://aha.pub/JoePhillips

_____

_____

_____

21

Are you encouraging your people
to do things 2–3 times faster than
they think they can? #GreatLeaders
http://aha.pub/JoePhillips

_____

_____

_____

22

You need to challenge your people to
the point they feel uncomfortable, if you
want to get the absolute best out of them.
#GreatLeaders http://aha.pub/JoePhillips

_____

_____

_____

23

If the goal is not challenging enough, your employees will think they can get there by working a little harder and getting a little luck. #GreatLeaders http://aha.pub/JoePhillips

_____

_____

_____

24

If you want big gains, help people have insights as to why you as an org need to change and do things differently. #GreatLeaders http://aha.pub/JoePhillips

_____

_____

_____

25

1 of 6 Challenges for the Organization: How to significantly increase the company's revenue. #GreatLeaders http://aha.pub/JoePhillips

_____

_____

_____

26

2 of 6 Challenges for the Organization:
How to significantly decrease the
company's expenses. #GreatLeaders
http://aha.pub/JoePhillips

_____

_____

_____

27

3 of 6 Challenges for the Organization:
How to completely transform the customer
base to increase ROI. #GreatLeaders
http://aha.pub/JoePhillips

_____

_____

_____

28

4 of 6 Challenges for the Organization: How to get all the players on the team more engaged and fully committed. #GreatLeaders http://aha.pub/JoePhillips

_____

_____

_____

29

5 of 6 Challenges for the Organization: How to effectively spread company awareness to the market you serve. #GreatLeaders http://aha.pub/JoePhillips

_____

_____

_____

30

6 of 6 Challenges for the Organization: How to attract and retain "A" players. You need a number of them in the org to succeed. #GreatLeaders http://aha.pub/JoePhillips

_____

_____

_____

31

Parkinson's Law: Work expands to fill
the time available for its completion.
—Cyril Northcote Parkinson. Do you
challenge time tables? #GreatLeaders
http://aha.pub/JoePhillips

_____

_____

_____

32

What is the Big Hairy Audacious
Goal (BHAG) that you're encouraging
your immediate staff to think about?
#GreatLeaders http://aha.pub/JoePhillips

_____

_____

_____

33

JFK had man walk on the moon through
a powerful vision, helping people have
insight, and they made it happen.
#GreatLeaders http://aha.pub/JoePhillips

_____

_____

_____

34

Don't be concerned if people think your goals are too challenging, as long as you believe they're realistic. #GreatLeaders http://aha.pub/JoePhillips

_____

_____

_____

#GreatLeaders look for ways to be more effective. They continuously teach & develop employees to do more.

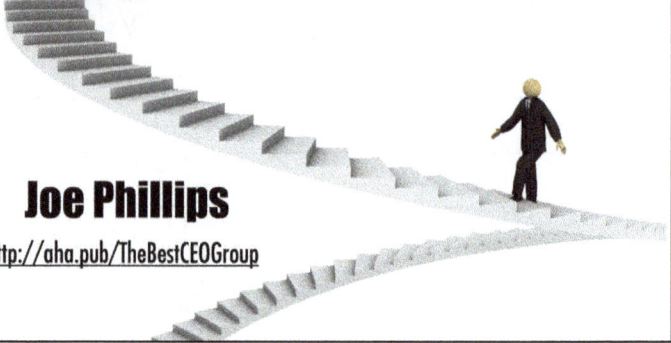

Joe Phillips

http://aha.pub/TheBestCEOGroup

Share the AHA messages from this book socially by going to
http://aha.pub/TheBestCEOGroup

Section III

What Is Required to Take
Your Business to the Next Level

Setting high expectations of yourself and your team is necessary to take your business to the next level. This starts with a clear, powerful, motivating vision that your team will rally around. So, let them be involved in developing it. Then, be prepared to make the investment to acquire the tools that the business will need to make the leap, develop your team, and recruit additional talent.

The business can only grow as fast as its people, so this usually means hiring talent that has been where you want to go and can help you get there. Also, it is important to have a group of people outside of your company who can help with your challenges and opportunities by offering suggestions and recommendations that you haven't considered.

35

Have a powerful vision and clear goals. Then make the necessary changes to take your business there. #GreatLeaders http://aha.pub/JoePhillips

_____

_____

_____

36

If you keep doing the same thing you do every day, you'll have the same results the next day. #GreatLeaders http://aha.pub/JoePhillips

_____

_____

_____

37

The CEO is generally the best person to bring revenue to the business. Have you optimized the business around that? #GreatLeaders http://aha.pub/JoePhillips

_____

_____

_____

38

#GreatLeaders look for ways to be more effective. They continuously teach & develop employees to do more. http://aha.pub/JoePhillips

_____

_____

_____

39

#GreatLeaders identify the opportunity of success & put out a plan for employees to help them have insights of what is possible. http://aha.pub/JoePhillips

_____

_____

_____

40

Do you challenge your direct reports
to delegate & empower others so
they are available to work on the big
strategies and goals? #GreatLeaders
http://aha.pub/JoePhillips

_____

_____

_____

41

To level up, you must think & act differently
than previously. @GrantCardone
via http://aha.pub/JoePhillips
#GreatLeaders https://goo.gl/GhqvCW

_____

_____

_____

42

Leaders need to develop trust through communication. Do your employees trust what you're saying? #GreatLeaders http://aha.pub/JoePhillips

_____

_____

_____

43

1 of 4 Things Employees Want to Hear: Things that give them trust in their leader. #GreatLeaders http://aha.pub/JoePhillips

_____

_____

_____

44

2 of 4 Things Employees Want to Hear:
That the business leaders have compassion.
#GreatLeaders http://aha.pub/JoePhillips

_____

_____

_____

45

3 of 4 Things Employees Want
to Hear: That the business has stability.
#GreatLeaders http://aha.pub/JoePhillips

_____

_____

_____

46

4 of 4 Things Employees Want
to Hear: That there's a bright future
with the company. #GreatLeaders
http://aha.pub/JoePhillips

_____

_____

_____

47

Don't just tell employees what you
want them to hear, but also get feedback
on what they understand. #GreatLeaders
http://aha.pub/JoePhillips

_____

_____

_____

48

Effective #Communication also involves being heard. Are you sure you are being heard? #GreatLeaders http://aha.pub/JoePhillips

_____

_____

_____

49

Have team-developed company values that are well known and used to operate the business and to hire. #GreatLeaders http://aha.pub/JoePhillips

_____

_____

_____

50

People who have shared values get along. People who don't will suffer through constant misunderstanding and conflict. #GreatLeaders http://aha.pub/JoePhillips

_____

_____

_____

51

#GreatLeaders have a game plan and get the whole team behind it to accomplish their goals. http://aha.pub/JoePhillips

_____

_____

_____

52

Don't be penny wise & pound foolish. This will cause you to miss many opportunities and stunt your growth. #GreatLeaders http://aha.pub/JoePhillips

_____

_____

_____

53

Make sure you have a buy-out clause with your partners, in case they don't help you level up the business. #GreatLeaders http://aha.pub/JoePhillips

_____

_____

_____

54

If you want to level up your business, realize that you and your team don't have all the answers. #GreatLeaders http://aha.pub/JoePhillips

_____

_____

_____

55

Have people around you who see what you're doing & tell you the truth. You may not like it but it's always helpful. #GreatLeaders http://aha.pub/JoePhillips

_____

_____

_____

56

When running an org your team has a vested interest in, they won't tell you the truth as much as you want. #GreatLeaders http://aha.pub/JoePhillips

_____

_____

_____

57

Want more business success? Seek a group of people who can support and help you be successful but don't have a vested interest in your success. #GreatLeaders http://aha.pub/JoePhillips

_____

_____

_____

58

Learn what your employees are good
at and ensure they spend most of their
time doing that. #GreatLeaders
http://aha.pub/JoePhillips

_____

_____

_____

59

Setting high expectations for you
and your team is the ticket to success.
#GreatLeaders http://aha.pub/JoePhillips

_____

_____

_____

#GreatLeaders make correct, tough choices. They must be able to "cut off a leg to save a life." They make these choices by understanding and caring for their people, not by following them.

Joe Phillips

http://aha.pub/TheBestCEOGroup

Share the AHA messages from this book socially by going to
http://aha.pub/TheBestCEOGroup

Section IV

Are You Doing What It Takes to Be a Great Leader?

Great leaders are not born that way. They develop over time through study, observation, and practice.

Leaders who become great are constantly looking for ways to improve their skills, trying new things and learning from their mistakes. They make decisions quickly and make them right. They know they can't do it alone, so they surround themselves with talented people who can help them. These people need to know the powerful vision for the business and the culture that the leader wants to have. It's best to involve key people in the development of both. That way, they will clearly understand and be committed to them. Then, the leader must set the example by living to these values and culture and demanding that others do as well.

Great leaders don't fight the fight, they direct the fight. So, if you want to become one, you should work on your business, not in it.

60

#GreatLeaders make time to work on their business. As opposed to spending all their time working in the business. http://aha.pub/JoePhillips

_____

_____

_____

61

Have you taken the time to step back away from the business and really look at it and what's going on? #GreatLeaders http://aha.pub/JoePhillips

_____

_____

_____

62

Life is a checkerboard, and the player opposite you is TIME. —Napoleon Hill via http://aha.pub/JoePhillips #GreatLeaders

_____

_____

_____

63

Great communicators help people have AHAmoments. These are the impetuses to drive action. #GreatLeaders http://aha.pub/JoePhillips

_____

_____

_____

64

The best leaders know they should get their executive team and other key players involved when deciding on the vision and other strategic decisions. Because that will get them more committed to those efforts. #GreatLeaders http://aha.pub/JoePhillips

_____

_____

_____

65

#GreatLeaders empower employees
to do as much as they're capable.
Are you empowering your team?
http://aha.pub/JoePhillips

66

When you say you are going to do
something, make sure you do it.
Otherwise, that will become the culture
of your organization. #GreatLeaders
http://aha.pub/JoePhillips

67

Develop a culture in your org that
when you say you'll do it, you'll do
it for everybody's sake. #GreatLeaders
http://aha.pub/JoePhillips

68

To be a #GreatLeader, you need to
be more empathetic and demonstrate
to the org that you do have a heart.
http://aha.pub/JoePhillips

69

Employees need to know they're
working for somebody they know, like,
and trust. http://aha.pub/TEDtalk via
http://aha.pub/JoePhillips #GreatLeaders

_____

_____

_____

70

Employees want to know that they're
doing something valuable in the world.
#GreatLeaders http://aha.pub/JoePhillips

_____

_____

_____

71

#GreatLeaders empower their employees to take on more than they are comfortable with, even if it leads to mistakes. Because this is how their people will grow and develop. http://aha.pub/JoePhillips

_____

_____

_____

72

If you prevent employees from making mistakes, you limit their growth and potential. #GreatLeaders http://aha.pub/JoePhillips

_____

_____

_____

73

Employees learn best by making mistakes —just be sure they don't make big ones. #GreatLeaders http://aha.pub/JoePhillips

_____

_____

_____

74

Star players are worth eight average employees. Are you developing or recruiting them for your team? #GreatLeaders http://aha.pub/JoePhillips

_____

_____

_____

75

Critical weaknesses are deadly. They must be addressed and fixed or the employees having them removed. #GreatLeaders http://aha.pub/JoePhillips

_____

_____

_____

76

Do you punish your good employees by giving them more work because they always get it done, while rewarding your poor performers by allowing them to do less? #GreatLeaders http://aha.pub/JoePhillips

_____

_____

_____

77

People trust leaders who walk their talk, live their beliefs and keep their commitments. Does that sound like you? #GreatLeaders http://aha.pub/JoePhillips

_____

_____

_____

78

#GreatLeaders make correct, tough choices. They must be able to "cut off a leg to save a life." They make these choices by understanding and caring for their people, not by following them. http://aha.pub/JoePhillips

_____

_____

_____

79

It's never devastating to cut a star performer who's a cancer to the org. The org always thrives. #GreatLeaders http://aha.pub/JoePhillips

_____

_____

_____

80

#GreatLeaders focus on their strengths, not their weaknesses. http://aha.pub/JoePhillips

_____

_____

_____

81

Identify where you have shortcomings and decide which ones are really important to address. #GreatLeaders http://aha.pub/JoePhillips

_____

_____

_____

82

As a CEO, if you have a weakness, delegate that responsibility so you can focus on what you're good at to bring more success. #GreatLeaders http://aha.pub/JoePhillips

_____

_____

_____

83

Effective leaders know when to
stop assessing and make a tough call,
even without total information. Little
is worse than a leader who can't cut bait.
—Jack Welch via http://aha.pub/JoePhillips
#GreatLeaders

_____

_____

_____

84

Ensure that you and your employees
delegate what you can, particularly the
stuff you're not good at. #GreatLeaders
http://aha.pub/JoePhillips

_____

_____

_____

85

Performance reviews with numerical ratings are generally demoralizing. You should be talking about things that get your employees energized and motivated to work on improving their performance. #GreatLeaders http://aha.pub/Joe Phillips

----

86

#GreatLeaders figure out what
their employees are strong at and
help them develop it even more.
http://aha.pub/JoePhillips

_____

_____

_____

87

Are you empowering your people to do
all the things they are capable of? If not,
you are limiting your business success.
#GreatLeaders http://aha.pub/JoePhillips

_____

_____

_____

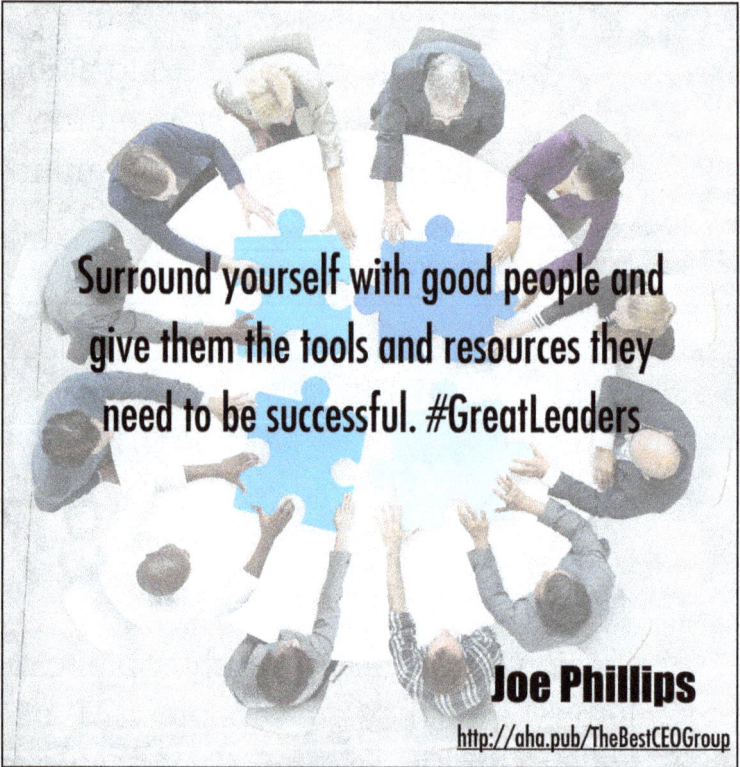

Surround yourself with good people and give them the tools and resources they need to be successful. #GreatLeaders

Joe Phillips

http://aha.pub/TheBestCEOGroup

Share the AHA messages from this book socially by going to
http://aha.pub/TheBestCEOGroup

Section V

You Can't Do It by Yourself;
Surround Yourself
with the Right People

There are people out there who tend to do things on their own. This approach has made them successful in the past, so they believe that's how they can achieve their future goals for the company. However, if you want your organization to reach its full potential, you'll need the help of others.

Sometimes, leaders are too close to the trees that they don't see the forest. This is why it's important to surround yourself with a good team of people internally, as well as externally. Listening to and considering their feedback and suggestions can give you invaluable insights you may have never considered.

88

Recruit and hire good people—not just those who keep the doors open, but most importantly, ones who challenge the org like you do. #GreatLeaders http://aha.pub/JoePhillips

_____

_____

_____

89

Hire the best people available, even if they're better than you; they will add more value to the company. #GreatLeaders http://aha.pub/JoePhillips

_____

_____

_____

90

Your business can grow only as fast as its people. At some point, it may be appropriate to bring in new talent that has already been where you want to go. #GreatLeaders http://aha.pub/JoePhillips

----

91

Success is a lousy teacher. It seduces smart people into thinking they can't lose. —Bill Gates via http://aha.pub/JoePhillips #GreatLeaders

_____

_____

_____

92

Surround yourself with good people and give them the tools and resources they need to be successful. #GreatLeaders http://aha.pub/JoePhillips

_____

_____

_____

93

Evaluate people thoroughly before bringing them into the company. This includes doing a minimum of two interviews, checking references, and doing a formal assessment. #GreatLeaders http://aha.pub/JoePhillips

_____

_____

_____

94

Getting a professional to go out and find the right person for your team can sometimes save you a lot of money. Are you using recruiters? #GreatLeaders http://aha.pub/JoePhillips

_____

_____

_____

95

Experience is a plus, but not everything. What's important is that applicants can do what you want, both today and tomorrow. #GreatLeaders http://aha.pub/JoePhillips

_____

_____

_____

96

Have you ever considered that the reason your business is not moving forward is because of you? #GreatLeaders http://aha.pub/JoePhillips

_____

_____

_____

97

#GreatLeaders participate in CEO or mastermind groups. They will give you insights you won't get from your team. http://aha.pub/JoePhillips

_____

_____

_____

98

#GreatLeaders have a group of cohorts they can depend on to give them brutally honest feedback and who are committed to each other's success. http://aha.pub/JoePhillips

_____

_____

_____

99

Have an advisory group that will
help you see things you don't.
Most leaders are too close to the
trees that they don't see the forest.
#GreatLeaders http://aha.pub/JoePhillips

_____

_____

_____

100

CEO groups are a great resource for
successful leaders looking to take their
business to the next level. #GreatLeaders
http://aha.pub/JoePhillips

_____

_____

_____

101

CEO group: like-minded people together, sharing tips & tricks for one industry and applying them to others. #GreatLeaders http://aha.pub/JoePhillips

_____

_____

_____

102

People in CEO groups generally get more insights from listening to other people's issues than they do from their own. #GreatLeaders http://aha.pub/JoePhillips

_____

_____

_____

103

Bring in the right experts to support what you're doing, where you don't need a full-time staff member. #GreatLeaders http://aha.pub/JoePhillips

_____

_____

_____

104

Bring on resources that could help you achieve your goals quicker. What's it costing you to not do that? #GreatLeaders http://aha.pub/JoePhillips

_____

_____

_____

If you don't hold your employees accountable, this will become the culture of your company, and little of significance will be accomplished.
#GreatLeaders

Joe Phillips
http://aha.pub/TheBestCEOGroup

Share the AHA messages from this book socially by going to
http://aha.pub/TheBestCEOGroup

Section VI

Why Leaders Are Often Disappointed by People's Performance

Have you ever been disappointed by one of your employees, followers, or friends? I'm sure the answer is yes. Most leaders have high expectations, and their followers often fall short of these expectations. But did you consider that in many cases, it may be your fault? Did you make it clear what you wanted or asked? Did they understand? And most importantly, did they agree with your request and fully commit to doing it when you wanted?

Thinking about your answers to these questions should give you some insights on how to get more of what you want.

105

Too many leaders don't praise for good work because that's what they pay for. They are missing a golden opportunity to reinforce what they want to get more of. #GreatLeaders http://aha.pub/JoePhillips

_____

_____

_____

106

There are 3 Kinds of Yeses people can give to your request: #1: "Yes, I hear you." #2: "Yes, I'll try." #3: "Yes, you can count on me. I'm fully committed." Which one do you usually get? #GreatLeaders http://aha.pub/JoePhillips

_____

_____

_____

107

Always ask for the "Yes" response you need, and make sure they give it to you in a formal commitment. #GreatLeaders http://aha.pub/JoePhillips

_____

_____

_____

108

You will get others to do what you want to the extent you help them have an insight that it is beneficial for them. #GreatLeaders http://aha.pub/JoePhillips

_____

_____

_____

109

Disappointed leaders often never communicate effectively how important a task is and their expectations. #GreatLeaders http://aha.pub/JoePhillips

_____

_____

_____

110

You get back from your people the behavior you exhibit, reward, and tolerate. #GreatLeaders http://aha.pub/JoePhillips

_____

_____

_____

111

If you don't hold your employees accountable, this will become the culture of your company, and little of significance will be accomplished. #GreatLeaders http://aha.pub/JoePhillips

_____

_____

_____

112

#GreatLeaders develop a culture of full commitment. Don't say you're going to do something without fully committing to it. http://aha.pub/JoePhillips

_____

_____

_____

113

Employees are more motivated by a leader's actions than their words. Are you properly motivating your team? #GreatLeaders http://aha.pub/JoePhillips

_____

_____

_____

114

When you ask something from your employees, make sure that your expectations are clear, that they fully understand the significance of the task, and that you get their full commitment to do it. #GreatLeaders http://aha.pub/JoePhillips

_____

_____

_____

115

You can't expect your people to do what they say if you're not doing it yourself. #GreatLeaders http://aha.pub/JoePhillips

_____

_____

_____

116

A #GreatLeader is one who not only says, "Here's what we're going to do," but also does it. http://aha.pub/JoePhillips

---

117

Should you expect commitment from your people if you don't fully commit to them? #GreatLeaders http://aha.pub/JoePhillips

---

118

When you are hiring people, ask them what the word "commitment" means to them and for examples. #GreatLeaders
http://aha.pub/JoePhillips

_____

_____

_____

119

If you are often disappointed in your people's performance, the cause of this problem is most likely you. #GreatLeaders
http://aha.pub/JoePhillips

_____

_____

_____

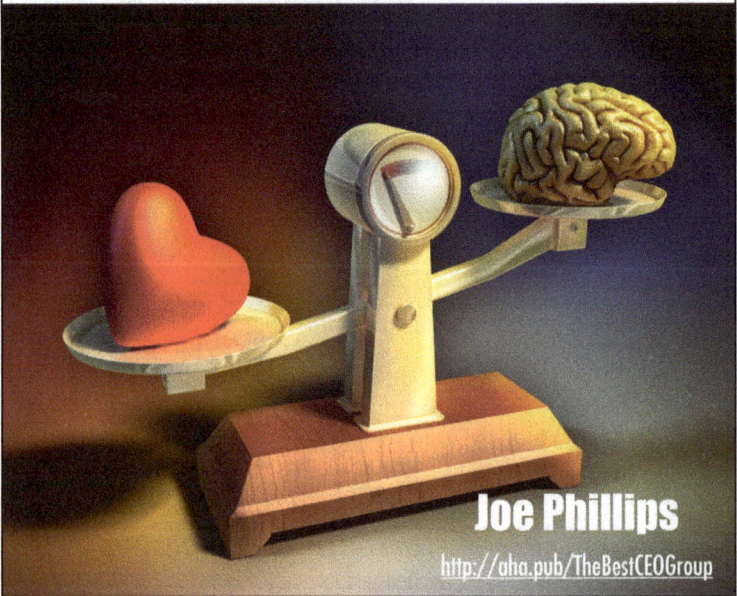

#GreatLeaders can balance the contradictory voices in their head between task and people.

Joe Phillips

http://aha.pub/TheBestCEOGroup

Share the AHA messages from this book socially by going to
http://aha.pub/TheBestCEOGroup

Section VII

The Best Leaders Have a High Level of Emotional Intelligence

When asked to define the ideal leader, many would emphasize traits such as intelligence, decisiveness, toughness, determination, and vision. Such skills are necessary but insufficient qualities for a great leader. Often left off the list are the softer, more personal qualities, like the ability to recognize one's own emotions, sense the emotional input of others, and react appropriately to that input. This is emotional intelligence.

Looking deeper, emotional intelligence consists of self-awareness, your ability to recognize and understand your moods, emotions, and drives, as well as their effect on others; self-management, your ability to control and redirect your disruptive impulses and moods and the propensity to suspend judgment until you have given adequate thought to the situation; social skills, the proficiency in managing relationships, building networks and teams; and empathy, the ability to understand the emotional makeup of other people and the skill to treat people according to their emotional reaction.

Numerous studies show that leaders rated in the top 10 percent display superior competencies in emotional intelligence capabilities, like: self-confidence and initiative, bouncing back from setbacks and staying cool under pressure, empathy and powerful communication, collaboration, and teamwork. These are all things indicative of great leaders.

120

Do you recognize and understand your moods, emotions, and drive, as well as their effect on others? You should because it can be so impactful. #GreatLeaders http://aha.pub/JoePhillips

_____

_____

_____

121

How good are you at recognizing your own emotions, sensing the emotions of others, and reacting appropriately to that input? These skills are critical for a leader's success. #GreatLeaders http://aha.pub/JoePhillips

_____

_____

_____

122

Leaders who can bounce back from setbacks and stay cool under stress are really appreciated by their team and generally get better results. #GreatLeaders http://aha.pub/JoePhillips

_____

_____

_____

123

#GreatLeaders can balance the contradictory voices in their head between task and people. http://aha.pub/JoePhillips

_____

_____

_____

124

Studies show that when it comes to top level leaders, 80-90% of the competencies that distinguish star performers are for their emotional intelligence. #GreatLeaders http://aha.pub/JoePhillips

---

125

Employees will stay with companies that are not all about the results, but about the people. #GreatLeaders http://aha.pub/JoePhillips

---

126

A relationship without trust = a car without gas. Stay in it all day, it won't go anywhere. @StephenMRCovey via http://aha.pub/JoePhillips #GreatLeaders https://goo.gl/j885CW

_____

_____

_____

127

What does it take to get your people engaged and committed to a high level? Good leadership. #GreatLeaders http://aha.pub/JoePhillips

_____

_____

_____

128

Leaders who have a good sense of the social and environmental systems in which they operate do consistently well in both the short and long term. #GreatLeaders http://aha.pub/JoePhillips

_____

_____

_____

129

#GreatLeaders know they can't have everyone on the team be just like them. Some conflict and difference of opinion is essential for a successful organization.
http://aha.pub/JoePhillips

_____

_____

_____

130

When employees love their jobs, they often feel committed to the organization that makes that work possible. #GreatLeaders
http://aha.pub/JoePhillips

_____

_____

_____

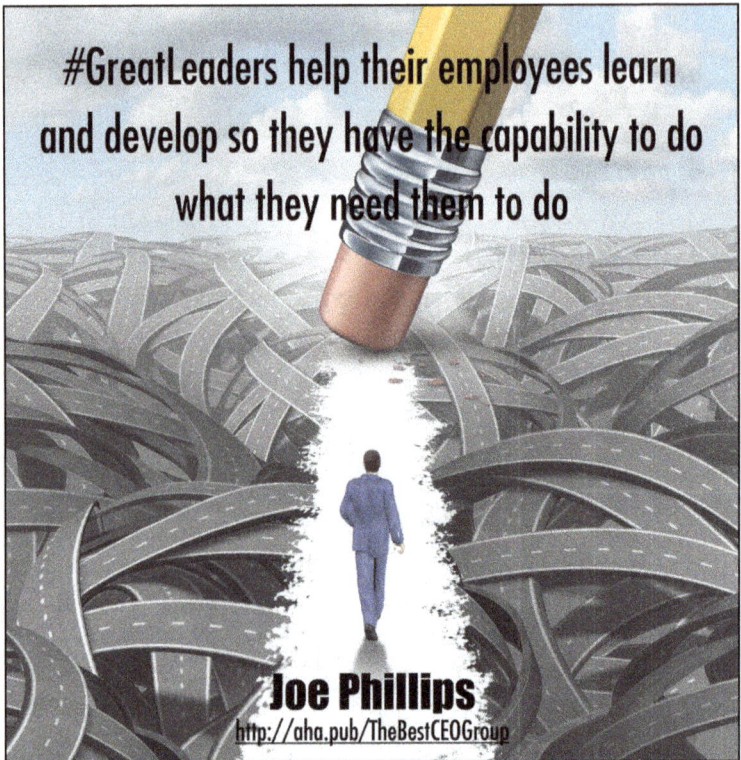

#GreatLeaders help their employees learn and develop so they have the capability to do what they need them to do

Joe Phillips
http://aha.pub/TheBestCEOGroup

Share the AHA messages from this book socially by going to
http://aha.pub/TheBestCEOGroup

Section VIII

Great Leaders Coach

Great leaders not only lead, they also coach. Problems are often encountered in the organization, which is why it's wise to prepare your employees to face these problems and have the capability to come up with a solution.

Most executives don't really see coaching as part of their job—they often just provide their employees with the answers. The problem with not coaching and just giving out answers is that your employees won't survive a problem without asking you for the solution and will always rely on you. They'll come to you all the time when there's a problem that needs solving.

Great leaders coach their employees and help them to have insights, not give insights to them. With these new insights, the window of opportunities opens and different solutions are now available, and the person grows. Over time, these new insights will make this person so much more capable to handle problems by themselves. This will free you up to do more coaching and other things that only you can do.

131

My job is not to be easy on people,
it is to make them better. —Steve Jobs
via http://aha.pub/JoePhillips
#GreatLeaders

_____

_____

_____

132

#GreatLeaders don't completely
delegate coaching to other staff.
They know they must personally coach
their direct reports and upcoming stars.
http://aha.pub/JoePhillips

_____

_____

_____

133

#GreatLeaders help their employees
learn and develop so they have
the capability to do what they need
them to do. http://aha.pub/JoePhillips

_____

_____

_____

134

#GreatLeaders ask insightful or thinking
questions that help employees come
to a conclusion themselves.
http://aha.pub/JoePhillips

_____

_____

_____

135

When you ask thought-provoking
questions, your employees will have
insights and see things differently.
#GreatLeaders http://aha.pub/JoePhillips

_____

_____

_____

136

When your employees have insights, they're more likely to take action, even for a thing they dislike doing. #GreatLeaders http://aha.pub/JoePhillips

_____

_____

_____

137

Help the people who report directly to you improve so they can take on more and do better. Are you coaching them? #GreatLeaders http://aha.pub/JoePhillips

_____

_____

_____

138

If you coach your team rather than give answers, they won't have to come to you as much but will take care of things themselves. #GreatLeaders http://aha.pub/JoePhillips

_____

_____

_____

139

Are you coaching and developing your employees so you can empower them to do more? #GreatLeaders http://aha.pub/JoePhillips

_____

_____

_____

140

It takes more time to coach people to have insight than to give it to them. But it's well worth it in the long run because they are much more likely to do what you want. #GreatLeaders http://aha.pub/JoePhillips

_____

_____

_____

Appendix

7 Challenging Questions to Ask

141

1 of 7 Challenging Questions to Ask: Who should be removed from your team? Most org have deadwood. Are you kicking the can down the road? #GreatLeaders http://aha.pub/JoePhillips

_____

_____

_____

142

2 of 7 Challenging Questions to Ask:
Who on your team hasn't kept up or
has changed your life? #GreatLeaders
http://aha.pub/JoePhillips

_____

_____

_____

143

3 of 7 Challenging Questions to Ask:
Do you have star performers who are not
team players and demoralizing others?
#GreatLeaders http://aha.pub/JoePhillips

_____

_____

_____

144

4 of 7 Challenging Questions to Ask:
Who are star performers who should
not be part of your team? #GreatLeaders
http://aha.pub/JoePhillips

_____

_____

_____

145

5 of 7 Challenging Questions to Ask:
Who in your org was a detriment
yesterday but not today? #GreatLeaders
http://aha.pub/JoePhillips

_____

_____

_____

146

6 of 7 Challenging Questions to Ask:
Is there someone who has a negative
impact, but you can't fire them?
#GreatLeaders http://aha.pub/JoePhillips

_____

_____

_____

147

7 of 7 Challenging Questions to Ask:
If you can't fire someone, how do
you prevent their negative impact?
#GreatLeaders http://aha.pub/JoePhillips

_____

_____

_____

About the Author

Joe Phillips is the Chairman of The BEST CEO Group. Prior to forming the Group thirteen years ago, he spent twenty-three years in the trenches, running businesses for others all over the world. As CEO of Western Digital Malaysia, Joe grew the business from $90 million to $1 billion in five years. He was a Vice President and Officer of one of the fastest growing start-ups in Orange County that grew to $144 million before being acquired. And he was recruited to lead the turnaround of three sick companies over a ten-year period.

Joe formed The BEST CEO Group to give back and to help a very select group of CEOs and business owners in San Diego improve their businesses, the bottom line, and make their powerful vision a reality. He knows we all make erroneous assumptions in our business, and that leads us to not considering some viable alternatives. If we were able to share our experiences and knowledge, be a sounding board, and challenge each other's thinking, we could shorten our learning curve and improve our success ratio tremendously. That is what his Group is all about.

Joe has an Industrial Engineering degree from Virginia Tech and an MBA from the University of North Carolina. He has offices and lives in San Diego, California.